Testing BI and ETL Applications wi automation approach

A comprehensive guide for Business Intelligence project evaluation

Published by Shanthi Vemulapalli

Version 2.0

Copyright 2015

Author: Shanthi Vemulapalli

Preface

The BI Projects are heart of the any business organization. The IT departments need to struggle a lot to bring them into a good shape by spending thousands of man day's efforts towards data validation, cleansing, transforming, consolidating and presenting to the users.

At the same time the BI Project evaluation for its implementation is a challenge to any IT organization. The resources should be well understood on its activities by collecting latest information. They also need to work in collaboration with the technical teams by understanding the latest design and development requirements. At the same time they need to confirm with the users on their understanding of the latest requirements before stepping into the evaluation process. This activity denotes lot of resource education is required for BI Projects evaluation.

One might get the following questions also into their mind:

Why do you need to evaluate thoroughly the BI applications?

Why do you need a Big Bang kind of test coverage for BI Projects?

Why do you need different environments for BI Projects?

What kind of testing is involved?

Is there any test automation process involved for BI projects?

By considering the above clarifications; with my past work experiences I have made this detailed E-Book to understand the Data warehouse concepts, development activities and the feasible testing methodology need to be used for applying the evaluation procedure.

After going through this document with clear understanding on it and IT professional can be ready to step into the BI project evaluation confidently. And he/she can demonstrate the performance well on DW/ETL/BI Projects phases.

Table of contents

Chapter1: Introduction

This document outlines a typical Data warehouses and Business Intelligence (BI) testing methodology and process by considering standard development activities. It also outlines the activities involve in planning and execution of the Evaluation project.

Background of Data warehouse and Business Intelligence

Databases and Database theory have been around for a long time. Early renditions of databases centered around a single database serving every purpose known to the information processing community from transaction to batch processing to analytical processing. In most cases, the primary focus of the early database systems was operational usually transactional processing.

In recent years, a more sophisticated notion of the database has emerged—one that serves operational needs and another that serves informational or analytical needs. To some extent, this more enlightened notion of the database is due to the advent of PCs, 4GL technology, and the empowerment of the end user. The split of operational and informational databases occurs for many reasons.

The Data serving operational needs is physically different data from serving informational or analytical need.

The supporting technology for operational processing is fundamentally different from the technology used to support informational or analytical needs.

The user community for operational is different from the one served by informational or analytical data.

The processing characteristics for the operational environment and the informational environment are fundamentally different.

The high level of this project can be predicted in the way of below chart for business understanding purpose:

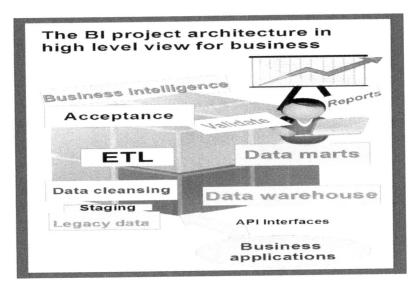

The minimal components are mentioned in the chart. From the below contents you can learn them in detail.

Chapter2: ETL

The Data Warehouse is the foundation of any analytics initiative. We take data from various data sources in the organization, clean and pre-process it to fit business needs, and then load it into the data warehouse for everyone to use. This process is called ETL which stands for 'Extract, transform, and load'.

What is Extract?

The first part of an ETL process is to extract the data from the source systems.

Following are the typical characters of the Extraction:

A) Most data warehousing projects consolidate data from different source systems.

B) Each separate system may also use a different data organization or format.

C) Common data source formats are relational databases and flat files, but may include non-relational database structures such as IMS or other data structures such as VSAM or ISAM. There are few non-relational databases like MongoDB. They do not need SQL to extract the data.

D) Extraction converts the data into a format for transformation processing.

What is Transform?

The transform phase applies a series of rules or functions to the extracted data to derive the data to be loaded. Some data sources will require very little manipulation of data. In other cases, one or more of the following transformations types may be required:

A) Selecting only certain columns to load
Example: Selecting null columns not to load.
B) Translating coded values
Example: If the source system stores M for male and F for female, but the warehouse stores 1 for male and 2 for female. There should be conversion process programs need to be applied.
C) Encoding free-form values
Example: Mapping "Male" and "M" and "Mr" onto 1.

D) Deriving a new calculated value

Example: sale_amount = qty * unit_price. There should be formulas in programs during conversion.

E) Joining together data from multiple sources

Example: lookup, merge, etc. through Database views or programs.

F) Summarizing multiple rows of data

Example: total sales for each region. Few queries need to be inserted in programs to extract the required data only.

G) Generating surrogate key values

Example: For different tables there can be common or uncommon keys. Those need to be analyzed for future extraction to pull the mapped data.

H) Transposing or pivoting

Example: Turning multiple columns into multiple rows or vice versa.

What is Load?

The load phase loads the data into the data warehouse for the below requirement:

A) Depending on the requirements of the organization, this process ranges widely.

B) Some data warehouses merely overwrite old information with new data.

C) More complex systems can maintain a history and audit trail of all changes to the data.

Chapter3:Data Warehousing

The Data warehouse as a collection of integrated, subject-oriented databases designed to supply the information required for decision-making.

Data warehousing is all about making information available. No one doubts the value of information, and everyone agrees that most organizations have a potential "Aladdin's Cave" of information that is locked away within their operational systems. A data warehouse can be the key that opens the door to this information where it should be available for the needed people.

Data warehouses are often at the heart of the strategic reporting systems used to help manage and control the business. The function of the data warehouse is to consolidate and reconcile information from across disparate business units and IT systems and provide a context for reporting on and also analyzing for the below needs:

A) Corporate performance management

B) Profitability

C) Consolidated financials

D) Compliance

The data warehouse provides access to integrated enterprise data previously locked away in unfriendly, difficult-to-access environments. Business users can now establish, with minimal effort, a secure connection to the warehouse through their desktop PC. Security is enforced either by the warehouse front-end application, by the server database, or both.

Because of its integrated nature, a data warehouse spares business users from the need to learn, understand, or access operational data in their native environments and data structures.

Chapter4:Data Mart (DM)

A Data Mart (DM) is a specialized version of a data warehouse (DW). Like data warehouses, data marts contain a snapshot of operational data that helps business people to strategize based on analyses of past trends and experiences. The key difference is that the creation of a data mart is predicated on a specific, predefined need for a certain grouping and configuration of select data. A data mart configuration emphasizes easy access to relevant information.

A Data Mart is a specific, subject oriented, repository of data designed to answer specific questions for a specific set of users. So an organization could have multiple data marts serving the needs of marketing, sales, operations, collections, etc. A data mart usually is organized as one dimensional model as a star-schema which is called as OLAP cube made of a fact table and multiple dimension tables.

What are the Reasons for Creating a Data Mart?

Following are the reasons for creating the Data Marts within the BI project.
A) It eases access to frequently needed data
B) It creates collective view by a group of users
C) It improves end-user response time
D) Ease of creation
E) It is lower cost than implementing a full Data warehouse
F) Potential users are more clearly defined than in a full Data warehouse

Chapter5: Business Intelligence

Business intelligence (BI) is a business management term which refers to applications and technologies which are used to gather, provide access to, and analyze data and information about their company operations. Business intelligence systems can help companies have a more comprehensive knowledge of the factors affecting their business, such as metrics on sales, production, internal operations, and they can help companies to make better business decisions.

Business Intelligence applications and technologies can help companies analyze changing trends in market share; changes in customer behavior and spending patterns; customers' preferences; company capabilities; and market conditions. Business intelligence can be used to help analysts and managers determine which adjustments are most likely to respond to changing trends.

Multidimensional OLAP tools are a major component of the BI decision-support tool suite. Terms such as OLAP, relational OLAP (ROLAP), multidimensional OLAP (MOLAP), decision support, multidimensional analysis, and executive information system (EIS) are all used to describe the exponential growth in the field of data access and data analysis tools OLAP refers to online analytical processing technology that creates new business information through a robust set of business transformations and calculations executed upon existing data.

An OLAP tool should provide a wide range of services. It should be able to support simple querying with just a few dimensions, and at the same time, it should be able to support powerful querying with many dimensions. In addition, an OLAP tool should be able to integrate all the analytical processing requirements of Querying capabilities, reporting capabilities, and multidimensional analysis and presentation of the results are some of the OLAP services that help turn data into useful information.

Chapter6:Technologies and Tools

There are different technologies and tools used in Data warehouse and Business Intelligence projects. The following sections outlines.

Technologies:

The below sub-sections explain the various technologies and their descriptions.

Source Systems:

They are the operational systems of the enterprise and are the most likely source systems for a data warehouse. The warehouse may also make use of external data sources from third parties.

Middleware, extraction, transportation and transformation technologies:

These tools extract and reorganize data from the various source systems. These tools vary greatly in terms of complexity, features, and price. The ideal tools for the enterprise are heavily dependent on the computing environment of the source systems and the intended computing environment of the data warehouse.

Data quality tools:

These tools identify or correct data quality errors that exist in the raw source data. Most tools of this type are used to call the warehouse team's attention to potential quality problems. Unfortunately, much of the data cleansing process is still manual; it is also tedious due to the volume of data involved.

Warehouse storage:

Database management systems (DBMS) are used to store the warehouse data. DBMS products are generally classified as relational (e.g., Oracle, Informix, Sybase) or multidimensional (e.g., Essbase, BrioQuery, Express Server). Few vendors only mentioned in the examples. Each vendor of the above tools might have several tools or features for handling the BI activities timely. Hence the reader needs to study on them further.

Metadata management:

These tools create, store, and manage the warehouse metadata.

Data access and retrieval tools:

These tools are used by warehouse end users to access, format, and disseminate warehouse data in the form of reports, query results, charts, and graphs. Other data access and retrieval tools actively search the data warehouse for patterns in the data (i.e., data mining tools). Decision Support Systems and Executive Information Systems also fall into this category.

Data modeling tools:

These tools are used to prepare and maintain an information model of both the source databases and the warehouse database.

Warehouse management tools:

These tools are used by warehouse administrators to create and maintain the warehouse (e.g., create and modify warehouse data structures, generate indexes).

Data warehouse hardware:

This refers to the data warehouse server platforms and their related operating systems.

Tools:

The below sub-sections explains the various tools and their descriptions.

Extraction Tools:

These tools are used to extract the data from the source systems.

Transformation Tools:

These tools are aptly named; they transform extracted data into the appropriate format, data structure, and values that are required by the data warehouse.

Data Quality Tools:

These tools assist warehousing teams with the task of locating and correcting data errors that exist in the source system or in the data warehouse.

Data Loaders:

The loaders transform the data (i.e., load images) into the data warehouse.

Database Management Systems:

A database management system is required to store the cleansed and integrated data for easy retrieval by business users.

Data Access and Retrieval Tools:

These tools allow users to make ad-hoc queries or generate canned queries against the warehouse database and provide exceptional responses to queries and typically have additional functionality or features.

Data Modeling Tools:

These tools allow users to prepare and maintain an information model of both the source database and the target database.

Warehouse Management Tools:

These Tools assist warehouse administrators in the day-to-day management and administration of the warehouse.

Source Systems:

Data warehouses would not be possible without source systems, i.e., the operational systems of the enterprise that serve as the primary source of warehouse data.

Chapter7:SDLC Activities

In any project the SDLC activities are mandatory for software development process. In BI projects also many components need to be built incrementally and test them. There are two types of SDLC activities considered in Data warehouse and Business Intelligence projects.

They are:

A) ETL development activities

B) Application development activities

Before anybody step down for evaluating the project outcome, they need to understand clearly the relevant development activities. Basically this kind of projects; are mixed with more percentage of ETL testing by applying white-box testing methods. Hence by having clarity on the development activities the testing team also can predict some issues. In the below sections the above two categories of development areas have been discussed.

Chapter8: ETL Development Activities

The following chart depicts the sequence of ETL Development activities and their flow:

The outlines of the ETL Development activities have been mentioned below:

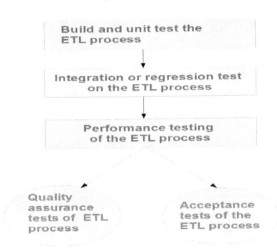

How to build and unit test the ETL process?

Under the direction of the ETL lead developer, the ETL programs must be developed for the three sets of load processes:

A) Initial load,
B) Historical load and
C) Incremental load.

If we plan to use a database management system (DBMS) load utility to populate the BI target databases, then only the extract and transformation programs need to be written, including the programs that create the final load files. If you plan to use an ETL tool, the instructions (technical Meta data) for the ETL tool must be created.

Once the technical components are developed for each unit, the ETL unit test plan need to be developed. The relevant test cases need to be developed along with the test data to break the code [if at all any defects can be fished].

What is Integration or regression test on the ETL process?

Once you have unit tested all the individual ETL programs or program modules, the entire ETL process flow must be tested. This activity is accomplished with integration testing on the first release and with regression testing on subsequent releases.

Both types of testing must be performed under a formal test plan with test cases, expected test results, actual test results, and a log of test runs. During this phase many data transformation issues can be found in 1st test cycle. Final output from this activity should be successful ETL Programs.

What is Performance testing of the ETL process?

Many BI target databases are very large databases (VLDBs), it is important to stress test the selected programs or ETL tool modules. This can facilitate to find some of the performance issues of the ETL Programs. The Final output from the activity completion should be the certified ETL Program library.

What is Quality Assurance testing of the ETL process?

Most organizations do not allow programs to be moved into production until they have passed through a QA test process.

This test is usually run under the supervision of the operations staff in a separate QA environment.

What is Acceptance testing of the ETL process?

Assuming Business representative and the subject matter expert have been actively involved in integration or regression testing activities, then acceptance testing should be little more than a final certification. If Business representative has not been involved, all functions of the ETL process must be validated to complete and correct, especially the reconciliation process.

What are the Data Transformation Activities?

BI projects present the best opportunity to eliminate dead and useless data because it allows the business people to see their information requirements in a different light. When properly implemented, the data transformation activities of cleansing, summarization, derivation, aggregation, and integration will produce data that is clean, condensed, new, complete, and standardized, respectively.

The below Figure shows the different activities involved in Data transformation:

The below content outlines the Data transformation activities:

Cleansing:

Cleansing is a BI transformation process in which source data that violates the business rules is changed to conform to those rules.

Cleansing is usually accomplished through edits in the ETL programs, which use table lookups and program logic to determine or derive the correct data values and then write those data values into the load files used to populate the BI target databases.

Summarization:

Numeric values are summarized to obtain total figures (amounts or counts), which can then be stored as business facts in multidimensional fact tables.

Summary totals can be calculated and stored at multiple levels (eg. departmental summary of sales, regional summary of sales, and total sales by country).

Derivation:

During this process, new data is created from existing atomic (detailed) source data.

Derivation is typically accomplished by calculations, table lookups, or program logic.

Examples include the following:

A) Generating a new code for classifying customers based on a certain combination of existing data values.

B) Calculating profit from income and expense items.

C) Appending the last four digits of a ZIP code based on the address in a postal lookup table.

D) Calculating a customer's age based on his or her date of birth and the current year.

Aggregation:

During this activity; all the data about a business object is brought together.

Example:

Data elements for a customer may be aggregated from multiple source files and source databases, such as a Customer Master file, a Prospect file, a Sales file, and demographic data purchased from a vendor. In multidimensional database design jargon, the term aggregation also refers to the roll-up of data values.

Integration:

Data integration based on normalization rules forces the need to reconcile different data names and different data values for the same data element.

The desired result need to have each unique data element known by one standard name, with one standard definition and an approved domain. Each data element should also be associated with its sources files and source databases as well as its BI target databases. Standardizing the data should be a business objective.

Chapter9: BI Application Development activities

The below chart depicts the various activities involved in Application Development.

The below content outlines the Application development activities:

Typical BI Application development activities

1. Determine the final project requirements
2. Design the application programs
3. Build and unit test the application programs.
4. Functional Test of the application programs
5. Provide data access and analysis training

How to determine the final project requirements?

Build a prototype, review the prototype results and determine what changes were requested and what issues were logged during that activity. This will give you an understanding of the stability of the requirements.

In addition, adjust the design or renegotiate the requirements based on what worked and what did not work during the prototype. Through this kind of proof of concept [POC] development methods, the users also can come to know the Data warehouse project needs.

The outcome of this activity should be Application design document.

How to Design the BI application programs?

While reviewing the prototype results and the required query and report mock-ups, design the access and analysis components of the BI application, including the final reports, queries, front-end interface (GUI, Web), and online help function. Develop Application test plan with detailed test cases.

How to build and unit test the BI application programs?

Create test data and write the programs and scripts for the reports, queries, front-end interface, and online help function. Unit test the programs and scripts not only to prove that they compile without errors but also to verify that they perform their functions correctly, trap all potential errors, and produce the right results. The outcome of this activity should be Application programs.

How to apply Functional Test of the BI application programs?

This activity is very critical for the entire BI project to certify the end to end BI application by following rigorous checks. From the below points one can find their importance.

Load the development databases with sample "live" data, and test the programs and scripts against them.

Check the actual test results against the expected test results, then revise and retest the programs and scripts until they perform as expected. Perform integration or regression testing on all programs and scripts in the sequence in which they will run in the production environment.

The final tests should be the QA test with the operations staff and the acceptance test with the subject matter expert and the business representative or users to certify them.

The Application program library should be the final delivery after this activity's successful completion.

What is the need to provide data access and analysis training?

Identify the training needs of the help desk staff, "power users," knowledge workers, business analysts, and business managers. Schedule the training sessions, either in-house or with a vendor.

If the training is provided internally, create the training materials and conduct the training sessions.

The testing team support on this activity is required since they are aware of the application functionality.

The outcome of this activity is the training material and the trained staff.

What is the environmental setup processes involved during development?

To support different types of ETL activities, organizations usually set up different development environments for different purposes. Following are the minimal requirements:

A) The prototyping environment: where the testing of the technology and the solidifying of the project requirements occur.

B) The development environment: where the programs and scripts are written and tested by the developers.

C) The QA environment: where the operations staff tests the final programs and scripts before allowing them to be moved into the production environment.

D) The production environment: where the programs and scripts run after being rolled out.

The prototyping and development environments are usually configured similarly, as are the QA and production environments.

The configuration differences are typically between the development and production environments. Key considerations appear below:

A) If the application works well in the development environment, there is no guarantee that the application will run equally well in the production environment.

B) It is conceivable that the migration costs from one environment to another could be substantial.

C) New or different tools may be required for differently configured environments.

Chapter10: Predicted issues in BI projects

In every BI project many issues will be there due to several situations. In this section we can see them along with the feasible solutions.

The below chart denotes the areas of the predicted issues:

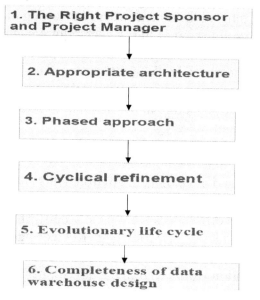

Feasible solutions on the predicted issues:

The below sub-sections outlines the feasible solutions against to the issues of ETL and Application development activities.

The Right Project Sponsor and Project Manager:

Having the appropriate leaders setting the tone, scope, and direction of a data warehousing initiative can spell the difference between failure and success. The management can look into it for a successful BI project.

Appropriate architecture:

The enterprise architecture team should verify that a data warehouse is the appropriate solution to its needs. If the need is for operational integration, then an Operational Data Store is more appropriate.

This verification activity needs to be completed before the BI project initiation instead of going for a reverse engineering process.

Phased approach:

The entire data warehousing effort must be in a phased approach, so that the warehouse can be iteratively extended in a cost-justified and prioritized manner.

A number of prioritized areas should be delivered first; subsequent areas are implemented in incremental steps.

Cyclical refinement:

Obtain feedback from users as and when each rollout or phase is completed, and as users makes use of the data warehouse and the front-end tools they can assess the output. Any feedback should serve as inputs to subsequent rollouts.

With each new rollout, users are expected to specify additional requirements and gain a better understanding of the types of BI queries that are now available to them.

Evolutionary life cycle:

Each phase of the project should be conducted in a manner that promotes evolution, adaptability, and scalability.

An overall data warehouse architecture should be defined when a high-level understanding of user needs has been obtained and the phased implementation path has been studied.

Completeness of data warehouse design:

The data warehouse design must address slowly changing dimensions, aggregation, key generalization, heterogeneous facts and dimensions, and mini dimensions.

Chapter11:Testing Methodology

The following Testing Methodologies and Testing phases are ideal for ETL and Application development activities. These were practiced and proven well with my customers globally.

The below chart denotes the typical ETL/BI Test methodology:

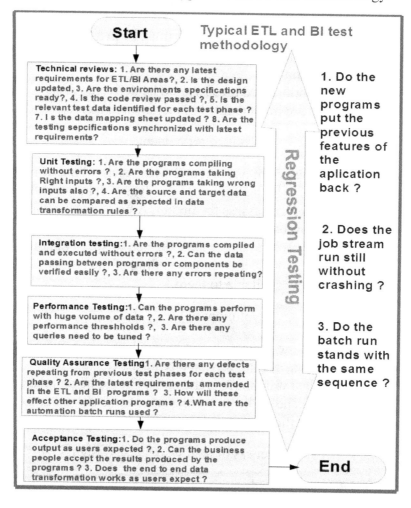

Methodology:

The following content elaborates the process and procedures involved in the verification and validation.

Unit testing:

It refers to the testing of discrete program modules and scripts. There are three components to unit testing
A. Compilation
B. Functionality
C. Edits
Let us see their definitions from the below sections:

A. Compilation: Obviously, each program module must compile successfully or it cannot be implemented. Tools allow the developer to trace every step of the code as it is being executed, displaying the before and after images of the data for each line of code.

B. Functionality: Each program module must perform the functions for which it was designed and must produce the expected test results. Unit testing is not completed until all program modules produce all of the expected results.

C. Edits: Each program module must catch errors and, depending on the severity of the error, either produce an error message or gracefully end the program. No program should ever stop abruptly ("crash" or abend) with a cryptic system error message.

Component Integration Testing:

Component Integration testing (CIT) is a testing phase which integrates individual software modules and tested as a group. The purpose of this phase to detect any inconsistencies between the software units that are integrated together.

This includes all three sets of ETL processes: the initial load, the historical load, and the incremental load.

Just because all program modules pass their individual unit tests, it cannot be assumed that the entire ETL process will run smoothly. The interactions and flow of all programs, as specified in the ETL process flow diagram, must be observed and validated.

Interactions: Program modules receive data, manipulate it, and hand it off to other program modules. This interaction between the modules must be tested. The test data used for integration testing is different from that used for unit testing.

Flow: The ETL process flow diagram should indicate which programs must run in which sequence, which programs can run in parallel, and where sort and merge utilities are interjected. This can be considered under a test documentation activity.

This flow must be tested for functionality and efficiency. Testing for functionality ensures that the right process is performed on the right data at the right time, that is, that the programs run in the correct sequence.

Testing for efficiency ensures that the entire ETL process can complete within the expected time frame. If it cannot, the flow must be redesigned, and the entire ETL process must be retested.

The business representative and the subject matter expert should be involved in integration testing. They are the first to know whether a particular run was successful or not.

Integration testing, like unit testing, requires many test runs to remove all the defects and to tune the flow. During these runs or test cycles; Every time the actual test results do not equal the expected test results.

Regression Testing:

The most complicated and most time-consuming of all types of testing is regression testing. It is similar to integration testing, but this time the programs that are being tested are not new.

The main goal of regression testing is to make sure that the modifications to existing ETL programs did not inadvertently produce some errors that they did not exist before.

Performance Testing:

Performance testing, also known as stress testing, is performed to predict system behavior and performance.BI performance testing is more complicated because of the enormous volumes of data in the BI target databases. Performance testing could be limited to only the most critical program modules with the highest volumes of data and the longest run times.

Quality Assurance Testing:

Most large organizations have strict procedures for moving an application into production. These procedures usually include QA testing, and in most cases a separate QA environment is established for such testing.

Acceptance Testing:

Acceptance testing can be performed in one of two ways, depending on how testing as a whole is set up.

If the business representative actively participated during integration testing or regression testing, there should be very few surprises during acceptance testing. In fact, if the business representative is comfortable with the integration or regression test results, and barring any unforeseen problems detected during QA testing, separate acceptance testing may not be necessary at all.

If a traditional approach was followed in which the business representative was not involved in any design or testing activities except for occasional reviews, acceptance testing is the most important test of all.

Business representative is involved in source data analysis and in providing the business rules for data cleansing, it is only logical that he or she should test the ETL process that implements those rules.

The business representative should ask some of the following questions:

i) Is the appropriate data being extracted?

ii) If the source data element is split into multiple columns, is it done correctly during the transformation process?

iii) If some data elements are merged together did any integrity problems result from this transformation process?

iv) Is the data loaded correctly into the appropriate BI target databases and the appropriate BI tables?

v) Can the data in the BI target databases be reconciled with the source files and source databases? Where are the reconciliation totals stored?

vi) Are the data values correctly transformed and cleansed? Is bad data slipping through without notice?

vii) Is the load performance adequate? And is the BI data available to the business people when they expect it?

Testing Phases:

In the previous section we have seen the different phases of the testing in SDLC.

Now let us see from the following sections; different phases of testing and their purpose:

Unit Testing:

Unit testing validates individual units of the application source code are working properly or not.

The purpose of unit testing is to isolate each part of the program and show that the individual parts are working correctly.

Component Integration Testing:

Component Integration testing (CIT) is a testing phase which integrates individual software modules and tested as a group. The purpose of this phase to detect any inconsistencies between the software units that are integrated together.

Quality Assurance Testing:

The QA testing is considered under Verification [QA] and Validation testing QC (VVT) is conducted on a complete integrated system to evaluate the system's compliance with its specified requirements.

Acceptance Testing:

Customer Acceptance Testing (CAT) is performed by the customer on a system prior to the customer accepting delivery or accepting ownership of the system.

Performance Testing:

Performance testing is testing that is performed to determine how fast some aspect of a system performs under a particular workload.

It can also serve to validate and verify other quality attributes of the system, such as scalability and reliability.

Regression Testing:

The re-run of tests is; with the intention of checking what was working is still working, after the bug fixing.

Chapter12:Checklists for ETL test planning

For project test planning, data collection is required.

The following checklist on different phases of BI project helps in data collections and test planning also:

Source Data Extracts:

1. Who will write the ETL programs? Have those developers' written ETL programs before? Do they understand the ETL process?

2. Do ETL programs already exist from a previous release or another BI application? How many of them have to be expanded?

3. Can we ask the programmers of the operational systems to give us the extract files, or do we have to get the source data ourselves?

4. What do we need to know about the operational systems before we can get the data?

5. What operational programs have to finish running before we can extract the data from the source files and source databases?

ETL Tool:

6. Have we worked with this ETL tool before, or is it new to us?

7. Has the ETL team been sufficiently trained on the ETL tool?

8. Can the ETL tool perform all the required transformations, or will we have to write some custom code? In what language (PL/SQL, Shell, C++, COBOL)?

ETL Process Dependencies:

9. What are the dependencies among program modules? In what sequence do we have to run our ETL programs (or the ETL tool modules)?

10. How many program modules can we run in parallel?

11. What are the dependencies among the tables? Do some tables have to be loaded before others?

Testing:

12. Will we conduct peer reviews? Are we using agile techniques?

13. How many testers will we have on the project?

14. Will the subject matter expert and business representative participate in testing?

15. Who will be the testing coordinator? Who will log the test results and maintain the test log?

16. What type of testing do we need to perform? Integration or regression testing? Performance testing? QA testing? Acceptance testing?

17. Which business people will participate in acceptance testing? Only the business representative? The subject matter expert? Other business people?

Technical Considerations:

18. What technical platform issues do we have to take into consideration?

19. How is the staging area set up? On a dedicated server?

20. Will the ETL process be split between the mainframe and one or more servers?

21. What environments does the ETL tool run in?

22. What type of middleware do we need?

What is Test automation?

In reference to the SDLC activities of ETL and real application S/W, there are various testing phases involved. Typically all these testing phases will have regression test cycles as mandatory to evaluate the quality of the code as well as application software, GUI interface.

There are two types of Regression-test automation methods to automate the entire DW/BI applications. They are:

Back end Test automation by writing source code with PL/SQL or Perl Script.

Front end application S/W automation by using standard and stabilized GUI tool.

As a part of test-automation methodology, the below sections describes the different activities involved in automation. The further section also explains their test automation development process involved as per standards.

Chapter13:Test Automation activities

In any BI project to do the manual testing from ETL to BI front end is a complex activity. At the same time even for a mall requirement we need to complete the regression testing. Doing manually this kind of activities across the Data warehouse interfaces is laborious also and the testing life cycle needs many man days. In such cases; we need to split them into different parts and identify to automate this verification and validation process. When we are thinking to plan for the automation, we need to identify some of the automation activities by following different process steps. This section is elaborating on these activities.

Following are the common test automation activities, and these activities can be considered as standard or usual feasibility study or tasks for every test step. With this process BI front-end only can be tested.

If you want to test the ETL Programs you need to make sure your ETL programs are running to bring the data into data marts. The data can be verified through tools configuration. There is a Database testing concept also in every GUI testing tools. One might need to write SQL related scripts from the tools native scripting language. If you are not using testing tools, you may need to use PL/SQL or some other scripting language which can call the Database tables.

You can use that concept to pull the source data and compare with the front-end received output. You might need to write some data transformation code also in tool's script for correct data comparison.

For planning the data verification, you can use the data migration practices those were mentioned in a separate chapter in this book.

Now let us see the process steps and their description:

Identifying the product features:

Every component in any application will be having standard features. These features will not change quite often. During this stage, these can be identified.

Test analysis:

Similar to the applications requirements analysis during the re-engineering, a test analysis should be done to identify the correct test scenarios and the relevant steps. During the test analysis many steps can be repeatable or they can be reused. The process related to these steps identification can be applied through the below sub-sections.

Identifying the test scenarios:

Under each standard [unchangeable] feature or sub-feature the test scenarios need to be identified.

Test case:

Please let us note each test scenario can have one or several test cases those will be denoting to use different combinational data to test a piece of information. Hence test cases documentation is also very essential for any project evaluation. Also let us make sure a product feature is decomposed into different test scenarios. A test scenario can have one or more test cases. And each test case can have one or more test requirements. Further sections will use these terminologies.

Identifying the repeatable steps in each scenario(s):

From the above identified test scenarios, we need to identify the repeatable steps.

Identifying the common repeatable steps for different scenario(s):

During this stage repeatable actions will be identified in different scenarios.

Identifying the repeatable manual actions for automation:

Within the repeatable steps, the repeatable manual actions can be identified. For example, the manual actions can be mouse clicks, clicking buttons etc.

Identifying the automation framework functions:

From the identified repeatable actions, the Test Automation Framework [TAF] functions need to be identified. These functions can be used for automation scripts development. These can be called as reusable functions.

Identifying the non-repeatable [one time action] test steps from test scenarios:

From the selected test scenario(s), we need to identify the non-repeatable steps.

Planning for designing the automation frame work functions using any automation tool:

Once the TAF functions are identified, the design plan can be made. During the design plan all these functions purpose and usage can be made.

Identifying the verification steps/points for any tool:

The GUI screens will have valid checks. These checks used to be performed during manual test.

Identifying the GUI objects on screens/tabs, etc.:

The property of all the GUI objects needs to be identified. The placement of the objects on the screen is verified.

Develop the test design steps for any typical automation test tool:

The design steps describing the flow of the screen operations are developed.
Identify the steps those cannot be automated, with the reasons:
The steps which can't be automated due to various reasons are identified and documented. For example, these might include drag and drop, print and other similar options.

Develop automation test design document with the above identifications:

Based on the above steps the automation test design document is developed, this document will contain the object details, the test design steps and the UI description.

All of these can be mapped to the test scenarios.

What is Test Automation Development Process?

After getting the clarity on the repeatable and non-repeatable steps from the test analysis, we need to transform them into automation analysis. During this phase by conducting an automation requirements analysis we can identify the automation requirements.

Chapter14:Test cases and requirements analysis

Most of the activities going to be performed are similar from the previous section. When you have decided to automate the testing activities you need to perform these activities again to make sure they meet the automation planning and design requirements. Another important note is if you have the repeatable tests for different builds then only those specifications can be used for test automation.

During the automation analysis phase different activities can be applied through the below chart under test cases and requirements analysis:

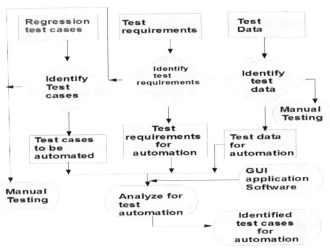

Regression Test Cases:

During this stage, the manual Regression scripts of the application should have been identified and finalized.

Identify Test Requirements:

Under this activity requirements will be identified which need to be verified during the testing process.

Test Requirements to be automated:

Once the test requirements identification is done in the previous stage, we need to identify requirements those can be automated in the regression testing process.

Test Data:

Assuming the manual test data is available while applying the regression tests.

The manual test data can be identified against to the regression test scripts.

Identify Test Data:

Test Data are data which have been specifically identified for use in executing test scripts, and are used to verify the expected results obtained, and these will be identified in this stage.

Test Data to be automated:

During this stage the test data which must be used during the script execution will be identified in automation process.

Assuming the GUI areas of these scripts will not have changes. They can be executed right away without changing the steps.

Identify Test Cases:

Following criteria can be used for identifying the proposed scripts for test automation:

A. They can be repeatable for tests in different test cycles.

B. They can save manual test efforts.

C. By using automation, we can cover more test coverage by enhancing/modifying the test data.

These scripts should not be used only for one time test execution in a release.

Test Cases to be automated:

During this stage the scenarios those can be automated during the automation process will be identified.

Chapter15:Analyze for Test Automation

Once the regression test cases and test data have been identified for automation, they should be mapped for the test steps/scripts.

If there are gaps in test data, they should be filled. Once the analysis has been done, further process steps can be considered.

The following content elaborates on test-automation development process.

Design Test Scripts:

At this stage, the proposed manual regression test scripts for automation should be analyzed.

The automated test design steps should be documented.

Design Automation Framework:

At this stage Test Automation Framework [TAF] functions should be identified.

The TAF functions can save lot of current and future automation development process efforts under reusability.

The future regression test suites maintenance will be made easier by the TAF functions.

With the application GUI or functional changes the automation scripts change will be minimal.

Develop Framework on models:

The Regression test scripts framework models can be identified using the design steps and identified repeatable functions.

These are related to:

A. Repeatable scripts.

B. Non-repeatable scripts

C. Data Driven Templates

D. Reusable screen objects

E. Reusable functions

Develop Scripts:

Any functional/Regression tool's initial stage will be recording the scripts, Hence the QA engineers need to record the scripts to identify the objects the application.

Code Review of Test Scripts:

After developing the automated scripts, code review should be performed, as a debugging process.

The code review on each automated script against to its manual scripts should be conducted with the below options:

A. By identifying the framework models.

B. By identifying the TAF functions.

C. By identifying the Data Driven Test Data.

D. By identifying the GUI screen objects.

Unit Test Scripts:

Once the Code review has been done on the automated scripts, Unit testing should be performed.

The following criteria can be used for carrying Unit Testing:

A. Combinational test data must be used.

B. The scripts should be configured in a different directory to test.

C. The script actions should be verified against the manual test steps

D. All the actions should be matched against the manual test steps.

E. Test data should be verified against the GUI screen fields.

F. The screen operation flow should be matched with the manual test steps

sequence.

G. Objects verification check points should be verified.

Sometimes there can more wait time, while executing script. It should be verified as per the expected results.

Prepare Regression Suite:

Once the automated test scripts have been unit tested and passed, they should be integrated into different functional groups.

Conclusion:

After going through this document with clear understanding on it; any BI professional can be ready to step into the BI project evaluation confidently. And he/she can demonstrate the performance well on DW/ETL/BI Projects phases to deliver the quality systems for the business.

About the author

Shanthi Kumar Vemulapalli is a seasoned professional with 25+ years of global IT experience in cost-effectively utilizing technology in alignment with corporate goals. Delivered bottom-line ITSM results through competent project and program management solutions, successful development and execution of systems, and implementation of best practices. He worked in different BI evaluation phases for more than 10 plus years for different business and technologies domain areas.

Recognized for inculcating a culture of innovation and knowledge sharing in organizations. Built teams for many companies globally; through training, mentoring and guiding the IT resources along with the on project competencies building. Supported for many infrastructure setups and conversion related projects [onsite/offshore model].

His Professional Certifications: ITIL V3 Expert Certification – Service Lifecycle, PRINCE2 Practitioner Certification, Lean Six Sigma Black Belt, Cloud computing Foundation [EXIN] and Certified Tester Foundation Level [CTFL].

He also wrote several blogs on the IT related topics.They are available in the below sites:
1. http://vskumarblogs.wordpress.com/
2.http://vskumarcloudblogs.wordpress.com/
3.http://vskumar35.wordpress.com/

Other publications: by Shanthi Vemulapalli

You can see from the following his other publications:

http://www.amazon.com/-/e/B018EDQTX6